THE WORLD ACCORDING TO
DODDIE

AN A–Z OF LIFE AND
HOW TO LIVE IT

DODDIE WEIR
with Stewart Weir

Illustrations by Jonty Clark

BLACK & WHITE PUBLISHING

First published in 2019
by Black & White Publishing Ltd
Nautical House, 104 Commercial Street
Edinburgh, EH6 6NF

1 3 5 7 9 10 8 6 4 2   19 20 21 22

ISBN: 978 1 78530 270 1

Design and Layout by Richard Budd
Printed and bound by Grafički Zavod Hrvatske, Croatia

*To Kathy, Hamish, Angus and Ben
and all those who have laughed at my
one-liners, especially those I borrowed
them from. A big thank you to Jonty
for his magnificent illustrations and
to Stewart, who has obviously listened to
me over the years and, better still, wrote
some of these lines down.*

INTRODUCTION

For years, travelling around the country and the world as a rugby player or when broadcasting, writing in newspapers or doing after-dinner speeches and the likes, people have said to me 'you should write these things down' or 'put that in a book'. And now I have.

They say you shouldn't laugh at your own jokes, but some of them are really quite funny. And how we arrived at some of these tales, one-liners, mantras and mottos, almost deserves a book in itself. The moments that make you think often leave a lasting impression and shape your life or career; learning by your mistakes, trying things once, and sticking to your opinions and beliefs.

However, sharing the good times with friends, family and team-mates, and the spontaneity which comes when you are having a good time, often with complete strangers, is something we've all enjoyed, and it's some of these wee moments I've tried to capture in this book.

I hope you enjoy them as much as I have!

Doddie
The Borders
September 2019

DODDIE ON . . .

ANATOMY

Someone once told me, 'I met you years ago –
actually I was introduced to your knee.'

AMBITION

Be happy for what you've got. Be happier for
what you've worked for.

"

AGEING
Daft laddies do grow up.

AUTOGRAPHS
Doing book signings is lovely, meeting people, but it's hard work. Put it this way, signature number 87 looks nothing like the first one you did. A selfie? Certainly.

ALWAYS
Always have time for others. If you don't, make it, especially for your own (maybe with the exception of my brother-in-law Dougie).

DODDIE'S
**POSITIVE THOUGHT
FOR THE DAY**

ASK PEOPLE YOU MEET,
OR KNOW, HOW THEY ARE.
THEY MIGHT JUST NEED TO
SPEAK TO SOMEONE.

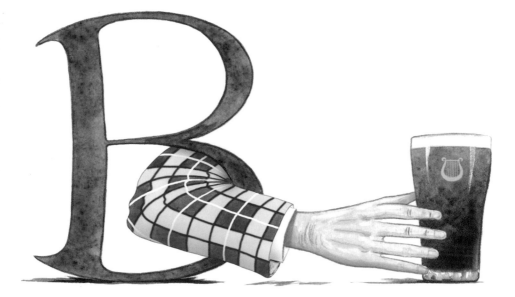

DODDIE ON . . .

BEER

It has been observed I could drink
a lot of beer. It did help I had a lot of
places to put it.

BEER

What is the daftest question I've been asked?
Probably, 'Would you like a beer?'

BEER

I WAS ONCE ASKED HOW MUCH BEER I COULD DRINK. I SAID I LOST COUNT AFTER THREE. 'REALLY, AFTER THREE PINTS?' 'NO, THREE DAYS.'

BOOZE

I WAS A LATE STARTER. I MADE UP FOR IT PRETTY QUICKLY.

BOND

We were filming at the Angel of the North and a woman asked why. 'He's the new James Bond,' said one of the crew. 'Oh I better get a selfie then,' said the woman. I suppose in the right suit, with some make-up, proper lighting . . .

BILL McLAREN

I'm not sure all the things Bill is supposed to have said about me are actually true. I know, because I've made some up.

BUILDING

People ask me where I get my tartan suits made. I don't get them made, I have them built.

BALANCE

They put warnings everywhere about how alcohol might affect you. Nowhere do you see it advertised that it 'may make you fall over'.

BULK

You never see a fat race horse.

There are certain skills you can practise in any sport, and that applies to rugby as well. But does it matter how much practising you do when you've muscled up and bulked up to such an extent that you have no movement in your arms or shoulders? That's a part of modern rugby I don't get.

DODDIE'S
**POSITIVE THOUGHT
FOR THE DAY**

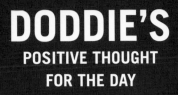

BE POSITIVE. IT'S AMAZING HOW MUCH BETTER YOU'LL FEEL IF YOU RID YOURSELF OF THE CLOUDS HANGING OVER YOU.

DODDIE ON . . .

CASUALTY

You don't play international rugby without making the odd trip to casualty. But if it's a bad one, you don't need a doctor to tell you.

"

CHRISTMAS

I was told I had MND two days before Christmas. Not something I had on my list.

CHRISTMAS

Christmas with young kids is wonderful, spending fortunes on the must-have gifts only to find that climbing in boxes and hiding under the wrapping paper is more fun.

CHRISTMAS

In an interview, I was asked to pick five highlights from my career. Number four was being sent to Lapland to visit Santa for *A Question of Sport*. They only printed three answers.

CROWDS

Someone asked me if I wore tartan suits to stand out in a crowd – I'm 6 foot 8.

CARAVANS

I was an avid caravaner once.
I probably held you up on an A-road without you even knowing.

CULTURE

My cultural skills came from Rob Wainwright. He taught me about all sorts: wine, whisky, cutlery at the dinner table. That you have to use it.

CHANCE

IF YOU GET A CHANCE TO DO SOMETHING, TAKE IT. IT MIGHT BE YOUR ONE AND ONLY CHANCE.

CHAT

In business and in life it's good to talk, even to rivals, in sport or business. They think you are being nice when you ask how they are, what have they been up to, what are they doing next. Really, you're tapping them for knowledge. Nice to be nice – even when you have ulterior motives.

COMPANY

I'm immensely proud of seeing my name in the tunnel at Murrayfield. Then I see some other names and wonder how they got there.

CARL, AS IN HOGG

He made me look good, both as a player and in terms of good looks. That cannot have been easy, but he achieved it.

COSMETIC

There are artists painting my picture and portraits now. It's fantastic. And, if you ask nicely, they'll perform some cosmetic surgery: tummy tuck, lose a few chins, pin the lugs back.

COST

That people remember me, years after I've met them, is nice. Means I must have been nice to them at the time as well. And as I've said, it costs nothing to be nice.

DODDIE'S
POSITIVE THOUGHT
FOR THE DAY

CALM DOWN AND HAVE A CUP OF TEA, OR COFFEE, OR A WEE GLASS OF SOMETHING STRONGER (OVER 18s ONLY; DRINK RESPONSIBLY). IT MIGHT BE ALL IT TAKES FOR YOU TO GET A BETTER PERSPECTIVE ON THINGS.

DODDIE ON . . .

Other people would dream of owning a Ferrari or a Rolls Royce. But I always wanted the biggest and best John Deere tractor. Nothing runs like a Deere.

DRESSING UP

I've reached a stage now when I wonder what I wore to dinners and occasions before tartan?

DRINKING

Drink responsibly – don't spill any.

DODDIE

My dad wanted the name George. My mum didn't like it. So I became Doddie and most people know me as that – except those who know me as Doddy, Dodi, Dobbie, Doadie or Doddee. Don't laugh, I've seen them all. I even got Debbie once at the pony club.

DODDIE'S
POSITIVE THOUGHT
FOR THE DAY

DON'T PUT OFF UNTIL
TOMORROW WHAT YOU CAN
DO TWICE TODAY.

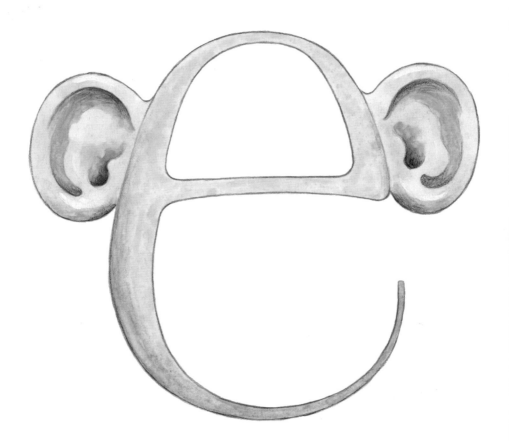

DODDIE ON . . .

EARS

When God was giving them out, I thought he said beers so asked for two big ones.

EDINBURGH

FOR THOSE ASKING, THE EDINBURGH MEDAL DOESN'T GET ME A SPECIAL LANE TO DRIVE IN. BUT IT SHOULD.

EATING

I DON'T THINK THERE IS ANYTHING I'VE NOT HAD ON A SANDWICH. I SHOULD HAVE GONE ON READY, STEADY, COOK.

ETIQUETTE

I used to raid our drinks cupboard at home, trying this, and that, and this, and that. I might have acquired a taste for it had I not put everything in the same glass.

EXPECTATION

Of everything I did in rugby, winning my first Scottish cap was the most cherished. Winning the second, third, fiftieth, sixtieth, equally cherished. Never took it for granted and never thought I'd made it. I just survived longer than others.

EDUCATION

Don't think because someone questions your qualifications that they are qualified to question what you might eventually achieve.

I'm thinking about kids leaving school here and how with all the pressure heaped on them to do well and pass exams, they are, at the same time, expected to grow up and have their future planned out. Really?

People got to know me through rugby, which led into media and commentary work, writing for newspapers and even a book, after-dinner speaking, motivational speaking, and now as an ambassador for my Foundation and talisman for the fight against MND. And in between all of those bits I sold lager for a living. None of the above featured when I was asked, 'And what will you do when you leave school?'

I'VE RECEIVED SEVERAL HONOURS AND ACCOLADES BUT THE ONE I'M MOST PROUD OF IS MY QUALIFICATION FROM AGRICULTURAL COLLEGE. FOUR YEARS TO FIND OUT HOW TO FEED SHEEP. BUT I DID IT MYSELF. IT'S ALWAYS GRATIFYING WHEN YOU DO THINGS FOR YOURSELF. AND THE SHEEP HAVE NEVER COMPLAINED EITHER.

ENJOYMENT

When you go to a party, or a function, and you've never been before, the temptation is to play it safe, telling yourself you've never been here before, best behaviour, drink soda water, say you're driving. Well don't. Bollocks to that. Have a good time. Just don't break anything. If you don't get invited back, did you really want to go there for a second time anyway?

EQUILIBRIUM

When we are out and about, doing Q&As around the country, folk ask, 'Who was your favourite stand-off: Craig Chalmers or Gregor Townsend?' I'd rather upset both rather than just one so I usually reply, 'Jonny Wilkinson.'

DODDIE'S
POSITIVE THOUGHT
FOR THE DAY

EVERY DAY, AIM TO LEARN SOMETHING NEW. HAVING CLEVER FRIENDS MAKES IT A LOT EASIER.

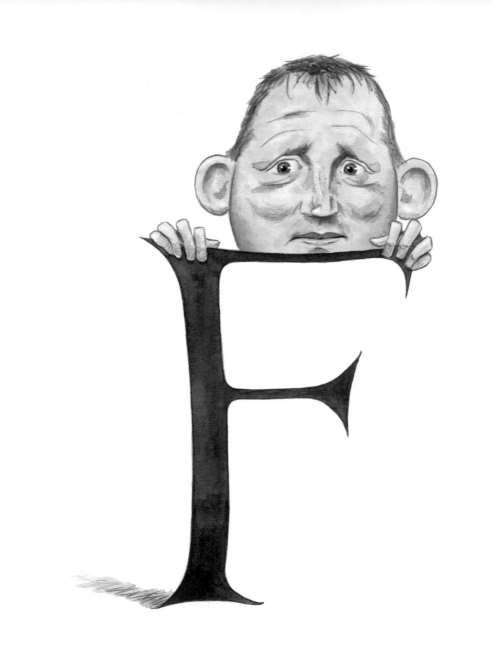

DODDIE ON . . .

FOOD

My mum, Nanny, was brilliant at mince and tatties. It was the only thing she could cook. So getting away with Scotland and the Lions was an education on new foods and cultures. There were times I should have packed Nanny up and taken her away, just to give her a few ideas of what to pick up at M&S.

FAILURE

You will fail, everyone has. It's hard, but it could mean you don't fail next time. And that would mean you had succeeded – and you will remember that long before any failures.

FASTENERS

I'd be worth a fortune if I had a pound for every time someone has said, 'Your button is undone.' It wasn't undone – it was never done up to start with.

FAMILY

THE REST OF MY FAMILY ARE
PRETTY NORMAL – I MEAN IN
TERMS OF HEIGHT.

FAN

I have become a fan of trains. Airport security – given my issues – is really difficult to negotiate. Just jumping on the train is so easy – and they regularly give you more time on the train than you've paid for.

FRIENDLINESS

Being nice costs nothing. Nights out, when you were with Scotland, either in Edinburgh or Cardiff or Dublin, cost nothing because you were nice. 'Can I buy you a drink?' Rude to say no – so I was nice and said yes.

DODDIE'S

**POSITIVE THOUGHT
FOR THE DAY**

FRIENDS WILL ALWAYS
BE THERE FOR YOU. MAKE
SURE YOU ARE AVAILABLE
TO DO THE SAME.

DODDIE ON . . .

GOD

Someone once said there are no atheists in the front line of a war. Maybe you need to be that close to your own mortality before you ask the question.

GOLF

In my day, I took quite a few difficult courses apart, literally.

GIRAFFES

I'll be honest, I looked at giraffes differently after Bill McLaren compared me to one.

GIN

I wasn't a gin drinker until I was asked to design Doddie's Gin. Now I'm a gin expert. Another fact that will stun people.

GOSSIP

Through social media, everyone knows what everyone else is doing, and even when you try to keep it quiet, someone will broadcast it to the neighbours. It's like the world has become Galashiels.

GLOBETROTTING

I've always loved travelling; going to new places, seeing new sights. Being a freak of nature, though, meant getting there and back wasn't always the easiest. Sometimes I wished I was there before I left.

GREATNESS

I don't mind being called a Scotland 'great'. It was great just to play for Scotland.

GOOD CAUSES

Why is there a need for charities? Take 10p from everyone, per week, and divide that up amongst all the charities. Revolutionary, eh? Vote Doddie.

GAMBLING

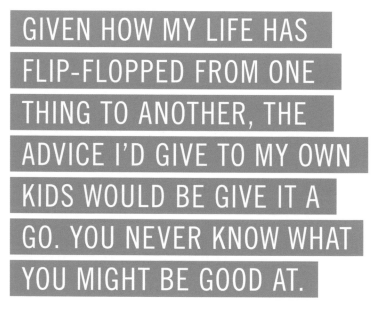

GIVEN HOW MY LIFE HAS FLIP-FLOPPED FROM ONE THING TO ANOTHER, THE ADVICE I'D GIVE TO MY OWN KIDS WOULD BE GIVE IT A GO. YOU NEVER KNOW WHAT YOU MIGHT BE GOOD AT.

My kids will read this and be saying, 'That is not what he said to me.' But it is what I was thinking.

DODDIE'S
POSITIVE THOUGHT
FOR THE DAY

GIVE SOMEONE YOU HAVEN'T SPOKEN TO IN AGES A RING. IT MIGHT BE GOOD FOR BOTH OF YOU.

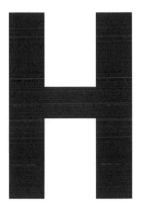

DODDIE ON . . .

HEIGHT

I am six foot six, or seven, or eight, depending on what you read. But I've never actually been measured. I said six foot six right at the beginning and someone believed me.

HOMELIFE

I THINK DEBATING SKILLS AND DIPLOMATIC SKILLS HAVE BEEN ERODED BECAUSE WE ALL NOW HAVE MORE THAN ONE TELLY AT HOME. WHEN THERE WAS ONLY ONE TV PER HOME, EVERYTHING WAS A COMPROMISE; NO ONE GOT TO SEE ALL OF THE PROGRAMMES THEY WANTED. NOW, EVERYONE HAS THEIR OWN TELLY AND DOESN'T TALK TO ANYONE ELSE. SEE, I'VE GOT YOU THINKING NOW.

HYPOCHONDRIA

People complaining about aches and pains
make me sick.

HOSTILITY

There are a lot of very nice people involved
in politics. Give them an audience, and that
changes. Is that necessary?

HORIZONS

It was always great going away and enjoying
new foods and new tastes – and always such a
disappointment when you came back here and
asked for the same thing which tasted nothing
like the original.

HOST

Never have a bad party. If you do, that's as much your fault as it is your host, or the people you've invited.

HONOURS

People talk about all the honours I've received; the OBE, the Edinburgh Medal, the university doctorate. I say all the honours? I haven't received anything for a fortnight now!!!

HOLIDAYS

The Lions is the pinnacle, once every four years, the best amongst your peers. Those reasons make it unique, special. And the best boys' holiday ever.

DODDIE'S
POSITIVE THOUGHT
FOR THE DAY

HEALTH, ESPECIALLY YOUR OWN, IS INVALUABLE. INVEST IN IT WHERE AND WHEN YOU CAN.

DODDIE ON . . .

I

There is no 'I' in team . . .
You don't want to do all the work yourself.

IMPULSE

Try everything once – unless it's illegal.
And if you feel you must, don't get caught . . .

IMPROVISATION

Nowadays I use a plastic beaker that's easier to grip. Some people frown when I go from wine to beer in the same glass. Why? It's all going in the same place anyway.

INFLUENCE

My favourite show on TV growing up was *The Professionals*; Cowley the old boss man, Doyle, Bodie. I always fancied myself as Bodie. Not easy when you are eleven, you can't pout, and you don't have a Ford Capri.

INTERPRETATION

When I was diagnosed with MND they gave me a list of things I should be trying to eat or drink, but they couldn't tell me for definite if changing my diet would work. So I amended the list to include red wine and Guinness.

DODDIE'S

**POSITIVE THOUGHT
FOR THE DAY**

IF IT HAS ALREADY HAPPENED,
YOU CAN'T GO BACK AND
CHANGE IT. SO PUT YOUR
ENERGY AND EFFORT INTO
MAKING THINGS BETTER FOR
THE FUTURE.

DODDIE ON . . .

JOBS

I've been an apprentice farmer, a beer salesman, a professional rugby player, a sewage tank salesman, an after-dinner speaker and now an author. I think I've been better at some than others.

JILL

Douglas . . . 'It's Jill with a "J", not "G" . . .'

JERSEYS

Folk tell me they don't see players playing for the jersey. But it's difficult to play for the jersey when the sponsors' name changes every other year. It might be nice, if you get a 4x4 out of it, or a lovely watch, or some nice beer or whisky. But DIY vouchers, or getting your dog wormed for free? Nah.

JOURNEY

I love the Borders. It's a nice place, nice people, not too close to the big cities, not too far away. And we've even got a train, from Waverley, last stop Tweedbank. No truth the only reason they built Tweedbank was so folk wouldn't have to get off in Gala . . . a nice story though.

• • • • • • • • • • • • • • • • • •

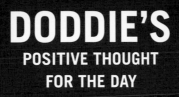

DODDIE'S
POSITIVE THOUGHT
FOR THE DAY

JOKES AND LAUGHTER WON'T BE A PERMANENT CURE FOR ILLS AND AILMENTS. BUT THEY SURE MAKE YOU FEEL A LOT BETTER.

DODDIE ON . . .

KNOCKS

I enjoyed rugby. It was why I played. As soon as I stopped enjoying it, I stopped playing. As a player today, I might not have started. Who wants to be making fifty tackles a game? Is that really enjoyable?

For me, you may take a few knocks but you've got to enjoy it. In work, you may have to do a job you don't like to survive. I get that. If you don't enjoy it, that's tough. But in sport, it has to be enjoyable, otherwise why do it?

KNIGHTHOODS

I'M NEVER SURE OF THE PROTOCOL WHEN YOU KNOW SOMEONE IS KNIGHTED. I'M TOLD YOU ARE SUPPOSED TO ADDRESS THEM AS 'SIR' — BUT SIR GEECH SOUNDS LIKE SOMETHING FROM GAME OF THRONES.

KNOWLEDGE

People say 'you must do a lot of reading up', or 'you must watch a lot of rugby on TV', so I know what I'm talking about when I do the commentary. I have a confession, I listen to other people and if I'm stuck, I phone Stewart Weir five minutes before I go on air. He knows some rubbish. But it's worked. I used to phone Gary Armstrong. But he took too long, looking for Ceefax or Teletext.

"

KILOMETRES

In today's modern game, I think players are maybe overanalysed. They are monitored about what they eat, drink, their weight. They are even tracked by GPS, where they are on the pitch, how fast they are, how many metres or kilometres they've run. I'd have just got my device and stuck it in Gary Armstrong's pocket.

KELSO

There are some very nice people come from Kelso, and even some clever ones amongst them.

DODDIE'S
**POSITIVE THOUGHT
FOR THE DAY**

KEEP BELIEVING. EVEN WHEN ALL APPEARS LOST AND YOU'VE TRIED EVERYTHING, KEEP THAT BELIEF.

DODDIE ON . . .

LAMBS

There is something satisfying, rewarding, walking about with a couple of newborn lambs down the inside of your jacket trying to get some heat into them. I'm surprised more haven't seen the potential as the ultimate country-scene fashion accessory.

LUCK

Like a lot of sport it's down to luck. You only get out of rugby what you put in. The harder you work, the better you get. Or, you can be like me: do the minimum possible, chance it, and hope you'll be lucky. It worked for me . . .

My good friend Carl Hogg worked harder than anyone I know in the game. Yes, he did eventually play for Scotland, but at a terrible toll to his body – and we are not just talking about his good looks here. I can say, with equal measures of pride and shame, that I didn't do half the work he did. And look where I got. That's luck – although I did make some of it myself.

LAZIEST DAYS

HOW MANY PEOPLE SPEND A DAY DOING NOTHING, THEN SPEND THE NEXT DAY REGRETTING THEY'D DONE NOTHING THE DAY BEFORE?

LAWS (OF RUGBY)

SO MANY LAWS HAVE CHANGED SINCE I PLAYED. NOT THAT I WAS TERRIBLY SURE WHAT SOME OF THEM WERE WHEN I PLAYED.

LOCATION, LOCATION, LOCATION

I'M VERY PASSIONATE ABOUT THE BORDERS. ALWAYS HAPPY TO HELP. NO TRUTH THAT I'VE IMPROVED TOURISM BY FOLK COMING HERE TO SEE IF THERE REALLY ARE DAFT FOLK IN KELSO, SELKIRK AND GALA.

LEADERSHIP

In the world of rugby you followed someone: a President, a blazer, a captain, a team-mate in front of you. That was how you travelled. When you left the rugby environment, it was a culture shock to be doing these things for yourself, finding your own way. Thankfully I had Kathy, or I'd probably never have got on holiday.

LIFE

People hear about someone suffering from MND and their thinking will be 'that's not going to end well'. But the bit in between the beginning and the end is someone's life – when every day means everything to the sufferer, and their family and friends. All I've tried to do – with the help of a great many – is make that part better, and if that means filling it with hope, then so be it.

LAST ORDERS

I have a rule at parties; you can't leave until you finish your glass. If anyone says, 'I'll have one more and then I'll go,' I serve it in a pint glass. Doesn't matter what it is, you're having a pint.

DODDIE'S
POSITIVE THOUGHT
FOR THE DAY

LIVE FOR TODAY.
THEN MAKE TOMORROW
JUST AS GOOD.

DODDIE ON . . .

MODESTY

How do you measure fame? In the Borders, there is no such thing; you don't even acknowledge the possibility of such a thing . . .

It's called 'staying grounded' in other parts of the world.

MARRIAGE

IT'S LOVELY.
KATHY, I'VE SAID IT.

MND

You've no idea the sense of achievement, the euphoria you felt, just doing up your shoe laces.

MEASUREMENT

I've got a simple rule; if you get invited back always deem your first visit a success.

MEMORIES

Why travel 12,000 miles around the world and then not take a taxi ride or a bus trip to see something of world importance. I know people who have done that. I've always looked at them slightly differently as a result.

MOTORING

I don't get worked up about Ferraris, or Lamborghinis, or Porsches in the same way as other guys do. But then I don't suppose they get excited about a John Deere tractor in the same way as I do.

DODDIE'S
**POSITIVE THOUGHT
FOR THE DAY**

MAKE TIME FOR YOURSELF
AND THOSE AROUND YOU.
IT MIGHT NOT SEEM LIKE
MUCH BUT IT WILL BENEFIT
YOU ALL.

DODDIE ON . . .

NATURE

Maybe it's my farming background, but I really appreciate nature: cattle, birds, trees. Wasps can be nasty and swallows make an awful mess, but you have to accept they are here for a reason.

(BEING) NICE

If you say you are going to do something, do it. Otherwise, say nothing. That way you don't let anyone down . . .

Speaking in Wales, a guy came up to me and reminded me where we'd once met; he'd been invited to hospitality with his wife and when they got there, there was only one seat. I met them in the foyer. Didn't know them, said hello and they told me what had happened. 'Leave it with me.' He thought I had disappeared back inside and that was the last he would see of me. But after five minutes I came back out and got him and his wife in. All I'd done was rearrange a few chairs. A wee thing, but sometimes it's that easy to make a difference, a difference people don't forget.

IMAGINE GETTING TO VISIT ROBBEN ISLAND, AND HOW HISTORICAL A PLACE THAT IS. ALL THROUGH REMEMBERING LINE-OUT CALLS. REMARKABLE.

NOMINATION

Being awarded an OBE was very special, although for a moment, I wondered if I should refuse it. You see, by accepting it, I couldn't say anything about Gary Armstrong having a medal for me serving the ball on a plate to him – and I couldn't be bothered rewriting my after-dinner routine.

DODDIE'S
POSITIVE THOUGHT
FOR THE DAY

NO ONE WANTS TO
FEEL POORLY OR ILL.
DON'T MAKE THEM
FEEL WORSE BY BEING
DISMISSIVE, NO MATTER
HOW BUSY YOU ARE.

DODDIE ON . . .

Spontaneity and originality is lovely. Try it . . .

The first 'Living with Lions' video was brilliant; no one knew what to expect, it was natural, not stage-managed. Since then, maybe not as good. You know what to expect, it's not been as much of a surprise. Try not to plan everything you do. Go with the flow – or to the pub.

OPTIMISM

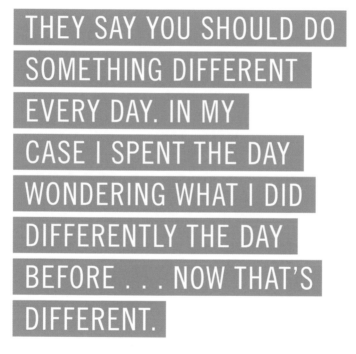

THEY SAY YOU SHOULD DO
SOMETHING DIFFERENT
EVERY DAY. IN MY
CASE I SPENT THE DAY
WONDERING WHAT I DID
DIFFERENTLY THE DAY
BEFORE . . . NOW THAT'S
DIFFERENT.

OPPORTUNITY

Always take the opportunity when it comes.
'. . . oh bugger. £1.36? I should have filled
up at home . . .'

*(While delivering one of my many mantras
to friends in the car, I find out the petrol
in Jedburgh is more expensive than in
Galashiels. Cost me a coffee that did.)*

OBSERVING RULES

Train is a more peaceful way of travelling,
especially the quiet carriage. Then a phone
goes off and everyone looks to see who has
disturbed the silence. All I can say is 'sorry'.

ORDINARY

There is no such thing as 'just a farmer'.
Those who just think that should try it for
a day, never mind 365.

OLD DAYS

The old playing-for-the-jersey scenario is lost
for me now at club level. How can you say that
when all you are doing is planning where else
you can go in two years?

"

DODDIE'S
POSITIVE THOUGHT
FOR THE DAY

OPEN UP OCCASIONALLY. GETTING THINGS OUT OF YOUR SYSTEM CAN MAKE YOU AND OTHERS FEEL MUCH BETTER.

DODDIE ON . . .

POLITICS

Next . . .

PALS

In times of adversity, pals will come to your door. Is that why I never see you, Stewart?

PRIDE

YOU CAN DINE OUT ON YOUR STORIES, ON WHAT YOU'VE DONE AND ON WHAT YOU'VE ACHIEVED. BUT BEFORE YOU CAN DO THAT YOU BETTER GET USED TO THE TASTE OF EGG ON FACE AND HUMBLE PIE.

PUNCTUALITY

Kids need looked after and tended 24/7,
365 days a year. Sheep are the same, although
they have an excuse; they don't wear watches.

POLITENESS

No, I was never very good . . .

*(My polite reply at a golf day when I was
asked if I would be playing – at an event
to raise funds for MND.)*

PHOTOGRAPHS

I'm quite happy to pose for photographs,
especially when we have some lovely ladies
in the picture beside me – I mean, I can get
my photo taken with ugly rugby players any
day of the week.

"

PLACE, AND KNOWING IT

Know your place. Not everyone wants to hear that, but on occasions, you just have to accept it – otherwise you might get nothing . . .

This refers to a trip when we went to Romania. We had decent seats, but the plane wasn't taking off unless the big, fat boys went to the back of the plane. So what was it going to be? – sitting in a not-so-good seat, or being remembered for having an international game cancelled because you thought you were too good to move?

DODDIE'S
**POSITIVE THOUGHT
FOR THE DAY**

PUT YOURSELF FIRST
IS WHAT PEOPLE WILL
TELL YOU TO DO. AND WHILE
THAT MIGHT NOT BE
YOUR WAY, SOMETIMES YOU
HAVE TO.

DODDIE ON . . .

QUEEN, HER MAJESTY

When I met The Queen for the first time,
I couldn't help wondering how many people
she had met during her reign. Will someone
have kept count?

QUALIFICATION

PART OF MY CITATION
FOR MY OBE WAS FOR
MY SERVICES TO THE
COMMUNITY IN THE
SCOTTISH BORDERS. THAT
WAS IN GENERAL, NOT JUST
THE PUB TRADE.

QUALITY

I don't know if I'd have one, even if I could afford it. £160,000 is a lot of money for a car. Why would you spend that on a car, just to fire through potholes and puddles, and to have it constantly getting dirty on the farm?

(Me on hearing I'd be chauffeur driven to the Lord Provost of Edinburgh's Burns Supper in a top-of-the-range Bentley Bentayga.)

(MORE) QUALITY

I'd have two – so I could drive one while the other one was being washed . . .

(Me after having been chauffeur driven to and from the Lord Provost of Edinburgh's Burns Supper in a top-of-the-range Bentley Bentayga.)

QUANTITY

It takes a bit of energy to lift a glass, so once you've got it up, you don't stop. Beer, fine. What I can say is that wine shouldn't be taken in half-pint gulps.

DODDIE'S
POSITIVE THOUGHT
FOR THE DAY

QUESTIONS SOMETIMES
DON'T BRING THE ANSWERS
YOU WANT TO HEAR BUT
IT IS ALWAYS BETTER TO
KNOW THE FACTS.

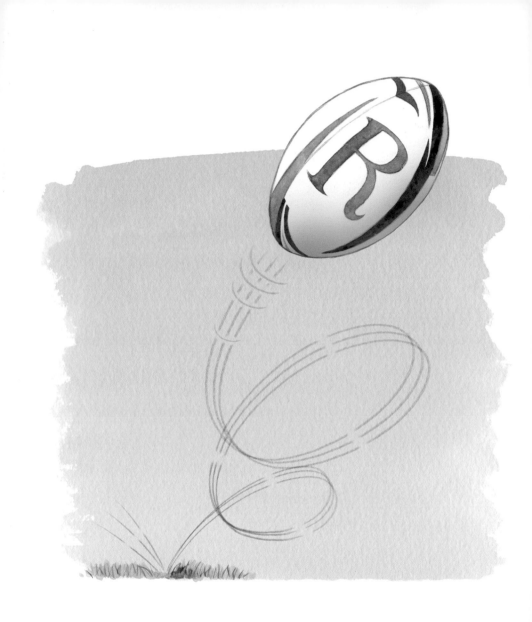

DODDIE ON . . .

RUGBY BALL

Nothing in the world has the ability to make
you look so completely uncoordinated and
utterly stupid as a bouncing rugby ball.
That, or an invite to dance.

RUGBY

I THINK MY SIMPLE PHILOSOPHY IN RUGBY HELPED ME PROGRESS MY CAREER. BASICALLY, IT WAS WHEN YOU GET THE BALL, GIVE IT TO SOMEONE ELSE AS QUICKLY AS POSSIBLE. WORKED FOR ME.

RUGBY

RUGBY HAS CHANGED; A PLAYER CAN NOW PLAY FOR 80 MINUTES WITHOUT TOUCHING THE BALL MORE THAN FIVE TIMES AND STILL GET RATED 7/10.

REST AND RELAXATION

I've been here for three nights – full board, and with a bed that fits . . .

(Me revealing to friends why I'd been unable to take calls after being hospitalised at Borders General Hospital.)

RELIGION

'Inga' Tuigamala once told me that he belongs to the church of Inga Tuigamala, so he believes what he wants to believe. I think with my issues, I've joined that church recently.

RECOGNITION

How do you measure fame? I don't know if it's just me, but I seem to speak to so many people – and so many people want to speak to me. Does that count?

ROAD RAGE

Have you noticed how angry some people get if you wave back to them?

REALITY CHECK

Living in the Borders has always been a great leveller. No one is great, only as good as the last time you played. For some, I never had a good game in my life.

RESPECT

I am amazed my Foundation has raised so much. Humble and amazed. I never thought it was possible to say 'thank you' to so many – and even then I might miss a few.

DODDIE'S
POSITIVE THOUGHT
FOR THE DAY

REMEMBER, DON'T BE
AFRAID TO SHARE WHAT
YOU ARE THINKING OR
FEELING.

DODDIE ON . . .

SCHOOLDAYS

When I went to school for the first few years
I wore shorts. Then I grew at such an alarming
rate that long trousers became shorts within
a few weeks.

SCOTTISH POLITICS

I played 61 times for Scotland, was stood on by every rugby-playing nation on the planet, yet got called 'unpatriotic' and a 'turncoat' on social media because me and other Scottish Lions backed 'No' in 2014. You learn something new every day.

SALTIRES

Someone asked if I had thought about getting a Saltire suit to go with my tartan ones. Eh, no. Hundreds of wee crosses would make your eyes go funny. And the elongated hot cross bun look is a definite 'no'!

(MORE) SALTIRES

The Saltire has to be one of the most identifiable flags on the planet.
It's nice to stand out.

SIBLING RIVALRY

I WAS ALWAYS BETTER THAN MY SISTER AND BROTHERS, AT EVERYTHING. IF I LOST, I HAD ALWAYS LET THEM WIN. THAT'S WHAT BIG BROTHERS DO.

SCHADENFREUDE

I'M SURE I HAD A PLATE OF THAT ONCE AND WASN'T IMPRESSED.

SOCIAL CLIMBER

The best thing about going on tour with Scotland, or going to the World Cup, or flying to South Africa with the Lions, was walking on to the plane and turning left. You really felt like you'd made it as you headed for First Class.

SEPARATION

I steer clear of politics where possible. In the last few years, for something that is supposed to be for the common good, it really has become divisive.

SPIRITS

It's one thing being positive but being positive can leave you so disappointed. I've always found that being negative to be positive worked for me. Sounds bizarre. But say you wanted to be picked for Scotland. I told myself it wouldn't happen. If it didn't, well that was what I'd expected. If, however, I got in the team, it felt twice as good because I never thought it would happen. I've done the same all the way with my MND. I thought I had it – and I did; thinking I might not be here – and here I am! That makes everything twice as good.

SNOW

People see snow and think Christmas,
skiing or fun. Farmers see snow and think
'twice the workload'.

STUPIDITY

We've all been there – if you say you haven't
you must think we're stupid.

SEX

That got your attention back . . .

SELKIRK

The best thing to come out of Selkirk?
To be honest, after the Selkirk Grace and
Selkirk Bannocks, you're struggling.

DODDIE'S

**POSITIVE THOUGHT
FOR THE DAY**

SOMETIMES THINGS ARE
BEYOND YOUR CONTROL. SO
FOCUS ON WHO AND WHAT
YOU CAN INFLUENCE.

DODDIE ON . . .

The first time I did TV and got make-up on,
I didn't wipe it off afterwards. I couldn't work
out what the girl behind the counter in the
petrol station was looking at.

TV

Once, in Ireland, I was asked to take my tartan jacket off because it was making the cameras go funny. 'What about the trousers?' 'We don't need your legs,' came the reply.

TV

When you do TV in a remote studio, and it's only you and the camera, that is quite freaky. And then people say, 'You looked a bit scared.' Try it!

TV

Appearing or performing on TV has never worried me. What my mum thought of my performance on TV, that worried me ..

99

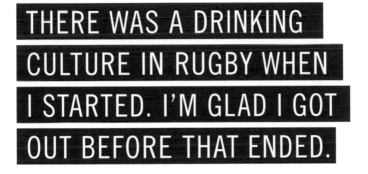

THERE WAS A DRINKING CULTURE IN RUGBY WHEN I STARTED. I'M GLAD I GOT OUT BEFORE THAT ENDED.

IS IT STILL A SELFIE IF IT'S SOMEONE ELSE TAKING THE PICTURE ON THEIR PHONE?

LIKE EVERYTHING YOU DO,
PRACTICE CERTAINLY
HELPS . . . EVEN DRINKING.

TELEVISION

Say yes to everything – then worry about how you are going to do it . . .

When I was younger, I was quite shy. To then, suddenly, be asked to do interviews for TV and radio, then appear on TV and radio as an 'expert' wasn't easy. But if I'd said no, I might not have been asked again. And that would have been worse than any on-screen failure. So I went for it – and the experience, and me, wasn't too bad.

TEENAGE YEARS

When I was growing up, you used TV to see what everyone else in the world was up to – and Saturday night was your big night for trying things out. Being a farm boy, I watched *Emmerdale*. That would explain so much about my teenage years.

TOM SMITH

Or Tammy Troot as I called him after the Lavinia Derwent books. Tom didn't have a clue what I was going on about.

DODDIE'S
POSITIVE THOUGHT
FOR THE DAY

TAKING PEOPLE FOR GRANTED CAN BE ALL TOO EASY. ALWAYS APPRECIATE THOSE CLOSE TO YOU.

DODDIE ON . . .

U-BEND

You'd be amazed some of the things you find in a U-bend. You'd be even more amazed what it takes to get them shifted.

(BEING TURNED) UPSIDE DOWN

There might be someone out there. I had a bad car accident, door flying off, on my roof, and survived. My brother-in-law died suddenly. Maybe someone is making those calls and has decided, with MND, that it's my turn now. From where I am, no one is putting up a convincing argument against that theory.

UPSET

What do I struggle with most? After buttons (which I gave up on a while ago), it's people being nice. They have the best intentions, but sometimes you have to say 'stop' and that they'll make you cry. And that is the truth.

I USED TO TRAVEL HOME FROM SCHOOL ON THE TOP OF A BUS, AND NOW THERE'S A DOUBLE-DECKER BUS IN THE BORDERS PAINTED IN MY TARTAN. THAT'S WHEN YOU KNOW YOU'VE MADE IT.

UNFULFILLED

The Professionals — that's where I got my love of cars. But I never had a Ford Capri, yet.

UNDERSTANDING

I never understood the saying about keeping your friends close but your enemies closer – until I started travelling with Gary Armstrong and Bryan Redpath. They weren't enemies, just so irritating. I think it's something in the DNA of a scrum-half, just to be annoying. And keeping them close meant you could see what they were up to. There is merit in that saying.

DODDIE'S
POSITIVE THOUGHT
FOR THE DAY

'UNTIL NEXT TIME' IS A COMMON FAREWELL. JUST TRY AND MAKE SURE THERE IS A NEXT TIME. SOMEONE OTHER THAN YOU MIGHT BE LOOKING FORWARD TO IT.

DODDIE ON . . .

VICTORY

'V' is for victory. Win, and the world is great. Lose, and that 'V' can be a message to you.

Victory in sport is so enjoyable. All the hours, the dedication, that hard work that has paid off. And the best part is no one counts how many beers you have afterwards.

VEGETARIANS AND VEGANS

THERE WAS A TIME IN MY LIFE WHEN I COULD NEVER REMEMBER IF ONE LIKED OR DISLIKED VEGETABLES. VEGANS? OH, THEY WERE A WARRIOR NATION ON STAR TREK.

VIEWING

Reality TV? What is that even about? I should strap a GoPro to my head. That would make interesting viewing.

VANISHING

I always thought a night out was a great way to bond, to galvanise a team, for you to learn who would help you in your hour of need, or who would go missing. If they could disappear on a night out, I always believed they could do the same on the field – the only difference being that you never got taxis on the pitch at Murrayfield.

VISION

MND is a dreadful thing. Me having it has meant more people are aware of it, are talking about it, are thinking about it and how they can maybe help bring about a cure or a change. That has to be good for the future.

DODDIE'S
**POSITIVE THOUGHT
FOR THE DAY**

VALUE YOUR TIME. BUT
VALUE THE TIME OTHERS
ARE WILLING TO GIVE YOU
AND YOUR CAUSES
EVEN MORE.

DODDIE ON . . .

WRITING

I did a book. Hasn't everyone? Now I've done two. I bet my old English teacher from school cannae believe it!

WRITER'S BLOCK

All authors suffer from this. I've been asked at book festivals how I cure it. Easy. I ring Stewart and ask, 'Have you thought of anything else yet?'

WHISKY

TAKING A WEE NIP OUT OF YOUR DAD'S WHISKY, WHEN HE LIKED WHISKY, WAS NEVER A WISE IDEA.

WEALTH

SEEING SOWETO LIVED WITH ME. WHEN YOU REALISE WHAT IT MEANS TO REALLY HAVE NOTHING. EVERYONE SHOULD WITNESS THAT.

WINNING

There was a time when the only winning you thought about was on the field. Now making a cup of tea is a 'Big W' as today's players call it.

WORK

I've been fortunate to receive a few accolades and awards through my MND work, and I did the same as a rugby player. But that's not what I did either for. It was about enjoying life to the full and making the most of your chance in life. What I see now are too many wondering what reward they'll get rather than putting the work in first.

WELCOMING

I've been humbled by people who have very little, but who have gone out their way to make me welcome. You don't forget that – you don't say 'no' so easily afterwards either.

WATCHING

Growing up on a farm, TV was almost our entire entertainment. And everyone watched the one TV, and everyone would have a say, or an argument, or a disagreement, but you'd all be involved. And it meant you had to speak up for yourself. Now, you can have four or five people in a house, all watching different things, on their own. No wonder people struggle to communicate.

99

DODDIE'S
**POSITIVE THOUGHT
FOR THE DAY**

WORK HARD, PLAY HARDER
– BUT NOT TOO HARD THAT
YOU CAN'T WORK AGAIN.

DODDIE ON . . .

XMAS

A poignant time of year. Each year I get to Christmas, it's another one I've put over on MND.

AMAZING, AREN'T THEY?
THE KIDS ASKED ME WHAT
THE EQUIVALENT WAS WHEN
I WAS GROWING UP. THEY
WEREN'T IMPRESSED WITH
BLOW FOOTBALL.

X FACTOR

I've heard people say certain players have the X Factor. I've heard them sing. Those folk are talking rubbish.

X-MEN

This was not what some of us needed. We have only just got to know the names of the Power Rangers.

XR3

I always fancied one as a kid, as a teenager. By the time I was 17 and driving, there wasn't one that was straight in the Borders. I had to imagine my Talbot Alpine was one. Two-tone, brown and gold. A babe magnet.

"

X-RAY

I've had loads of X-rays and scans and the likes.
They always tell you to lie still and not move.
How much nicer it would be if they just said
'smile'.

XXL

You know what they say about
big shoes . . . big feet.

DODDIE'S
POSITIVE THOUGHT
FOR THE DAY

XBOX, MOBILE PHONES, TABLETS AND GADGETS ALL GET IN THE WAY OF JUST SIMPLY TALKING TO THOSE AROUND YOU. SO, PUT THEM DOWN AND TRY TALKING. IT'S MUCH MORE REWARDING.

DODDIE ON . . .

YELLOW

Yellow cards? In rugby they are simply
an occupational hazard.

YOU

'You look like Doddie Weir – he wears tartan
suits as well.' I've had that a few times.
Al Kellock and my brother Tom have also
been mistaken for me. Some folk should
go to Specsavers.

YESTERDAY

Do what you can today and worry about
tomorrow when it comes.

YAPPING

There are some people who are quite
withdrawn, and keep themselves to themselves.
Then there is Kenny Logan who talks non-stop,
from when he wakes up till bedtime.
Then he talks in his sleep.

YOUTH

When you are young, you don't realise you are
getting old. As you get older, you realise all the
things you never thought about when you were
young. When do you cross that line between
young and old?

DODDIE'S
POSITIVE THOUGHT
FOR THE DAY

YOU SHOULD SET YOURSELF TARGETS, EVERY DAY, EVERY WEEK. MAKES EVEN LITTLE THINGS FEEL LIKE A MAJOR ACHIEVEMENT.

DODDIE ON . . .

ZOOS

If the late, great Bill McLaren hadn't likened me
to a giraffe in his commentary all those years
ago I might never have been famous.

(NEW) ZEALAND

I've been there but often wondered if an
old Zealand came first?

ZERO

People asked me what must it have been like for Scotland to trail 31–0 at Twickenham in the Calcutta Cup game and come back. I said I didn't know – I'd never been in a team that had been 31–0 down.

ZODIAC

Imagine how it felt to catch sight of the astrologist column in the paper who says your lucky number is 9 and your lucky colour is green when you are playing Ireland and you are the Scotland number 5?

DODDIE'S
POSITIVE THOUGHT
FOR THE DAY

ZLATAN IBRAHIMOVIC, THE GREAT
PHILOSOPHER AND FOOTBALLER,
ONCE SAID, 'I CAN'T HELP BUT
LAUGH AT HOW PERFECT I AM.'
BE LIKE ZLATAN: HAVE A BLOODY
GOOD GIGGLE TO YOURSELF!

SO THAT'S MY A–Z OF LIFE AND HOW
TO LIVE IT. I HOPE YOU'VE HAD A BIT
OF A LAUGH, MAYBE A WEE CRY AND
HAVE TAKEN ON SOME OF MY OWN
POSITIVE THINKING. WHATEVER
YOUR SITUATION, MAKE THE MOST
YOU CAN OF EACH AND EVERY DAY,
BE NICE TO PEOPLE AND LAUGH AS
MUCH AS POSSIBLE.

AND WHEN LIFE GIVES YOU LEMONS,
POP THEM INTO A LARGE G&T. I HAVE
MY OWN GIN NOW, YOU KNOW . . .

CHEERS!
DODDIE